W9-CPB-920

PICTURE WINDOW BOOKS
World Atlases

ATLAS of
Europe

by Karen Foster

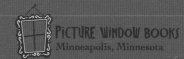

PICTURE WINDOW BOOKS
Minneapolis, Minnesota

First American edition published in 2008 by
Picture Window Books
151 Good Counsel Drive
P.O. Box 669
Mankato, MN 56002-0669
877-845-8392
www.picturewindowbooks.com

Editor: Jill Kalz
Designer: Hilary Wacholz
Page Production: Melissa Kes
Art Director: Nathan Gassman
Associate Managing Editor: Christianne Jones
Cartographer: XNR Productions, Inc. (13, 15, 17, 19)

Editor and Compiler: Karen Foster
Factual Researcher: Joe Josephs
Designers: Fanny Masters & Maia Terry
Picture Researcher: Diana Morris
Illustrators: Rebecca Elliott and Q2 Media
Maps: Geo-Innovations UK

Printed in the United States of America.

 All books published by Picture Window Books
are manufactured with paper containing at least
10 percent post-consumer waste.

Foster, Karen.
Atlas of Europe / by Karen Foster. – Minneapolis, MN : Picture Window Books, 2008.
32 p. : col. ill., col. maps ; cm. – (Picture Window Books world atlases).
2-4
2-4.
Includes index and glossary.
ISBN 978-1-4048-3882-6 (library binding)
ISBN 978-1-4048-3890-1 (paperback)
1. Maps-Juvenile literature 2. Europe-Geography-Juvenile literature. 3. Europe-Maps
for children.
D900   914 REF
                                                                 DLC

Photo Credits:
Arvind Balaraman/Shutterstock: 23tr; Derek Cattan/Corbis: 19b; Macduff Everton/ImageWorks/Topfoto: 12tr; Owen Franken/
Corbis: 18tr; Roland Gerits/zefa/Corbis: 8bl; James R. Hearn/Shutterstock: 26b; HIP/Topfoto: 9bl, 26t; Gavriel Jecan/Corbis:
18bl; Kondrashov Mikhail Evgenevich/Shutterstock: 18br; Oleg Kozlov/Shutterstock: 9br; Kurt/Dreamstime: compass rose on 4,
7, 9, 11, 13, 15, 17, 19, 25, 27; Tony Kwan/Shutterstock: 23cr; David MacFarlane/Shutterstock: 10r; Boyd Norton/ImageWorks/
Topfoto: 10tr; Picturepoint/Topham: 20bl, 20tr; Norman Pogson/Shutterstock: 21b; Vova Pomortzeff/Shutterstock: 23br;
Vittorino Rastelli/Corbis: 21tl; Ria Novosti/Topfoto: 27b; Eddy Risch/epa/Corbis: 20br; Louie Schoeman/Shutterstock: 10bl;
Gregor M. Schmidt/Corbis: 22br; Paul Seheult/Eye Ubiquitous/Corbis: 23cl; Shutterstock: 24, 25; Paul A Souders/Corbis:
11t; Jan Stadelmyer/Shutterstock: 23tl; UPPA/Topfoto: 6r; Woodmansterne/Topfoto: 8t; Adam Woolfitt/Robert Harding World
Imagery/Corbis: 22t; Michael S. Yamashita/Corbis: 21tr, 28-29.

Editor's Note: The maps in this book were created with the Miller projection.

Table of Contents

Welcome to Europe

The world is made up of five oceans and seven chunks of land called continents: North America, South America, Antarctica, Europe, Africa, Asia, and Australia. This map shows Europe's position in the world.

The Arctic Circle is an imaginary line in the northern part of the world that marks the edge of the Arctic region.

Arctic Circle

NORTH AMERICA

Atlantic Ocean

Tropic of Cancer

Pacific Ocean

Equator

SOUTH AMERICA

Tropic of Capricorn

Legend
A legend tells you the title of a map and what the map's symbols mean.

SOUTH AMERICA	Continent
Pacific Ocean	Ocean

Antarctic Circle

The Antarctic Circle is an imaginary line in the southern part of the world that marks the edge of the Antarctic region.

Compass Rose
A compass rose shows you the four cardinal directions: north (N), south (S), east (E), and west (W).

4

Europe is the world's second-smallest continent (after Australia). It is surrounded by water on three sides. The Arctic Ocean, the Atlantic Ocean, and five large seas border Europe. The continent shares its eastern border with Asia.

North Pole

Arctic Ocean

Arctic Circle

EUROPE

ASIA

The Tropic of Cancer and the Tropic of Capricorn are imaginary lines north and south of the equator. Places that lie between the two lines are hot and wet.

Tropic of Cancer

Pacific Ocean

AFRICA

Indian Ocean

Equator

The equator is an imaginary line around the middle of the world.

AUSTRALIA

Tropic of Capricorn

Southern Ocean

Antarctic Circle

ANTARCTICA

Scale Bar

A scale bar helps measure distance. It tells you the difference between distances on a map and the actual distances on Earth's surface.

Miles
0   0.5   1   1.5   2   2.5

0   1   2   3   4
Kilometers

South Pole

5

Countries

Europe is made up of 44 countries. Each has its own way of life and, often, its own language, too.

Russia is Europe's (and the world's) largest country, although only part of it is in Europe. The rest of the country stretches east across the Asian continent.

Europe's smallest country lies within the city of Rome, Italy. Called Vatican City, the tiny country has about 900 people. It measures just 0.2 square miles (0.52 square kilometers).

What's on the menu?

England – fish and chips

France – onion soup

Germany – sausage and sauerkraut

Greece – minty yogurt and cucumber dip

Hungary – spicy goulash and dumplings

Italy – four seasons pizza

Poland – gingerbread

Romania – cabbage-wrapped meat rolls

Russia – blintzes and caviar

Spain – paella

Sweden – pickled herring and crayfish

Up North

The Nordic countries include Denmark, Sweden, Norway, Finland, and the island of Iceland. Because of the region's cold climate, these countries have some of the smallest numbers of people in Europe.

ANDORRA   AUSTRIA   BELARUS

BELGIUM   BOSNIA & HERZEGOVINA   BULGARIA

CROATIA   CZECH REPUBLIC   DENMARK

ESTONIA   FINLAND   FRANCE

GERMANY   GREECE   HUNGARY

ICELAND   IRELAND   ITALY

LATVIA   LIECHTENSTEIN   LITHUANIA

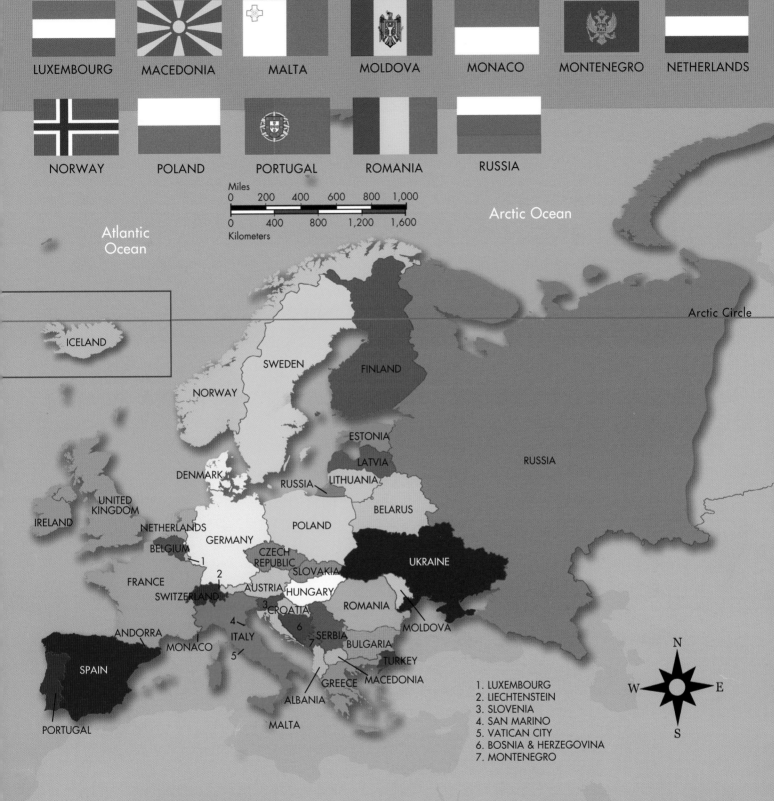

LUXEMBOURG   MACEDONIA   MALTA   MOLDOVA   MONACO   MONTENEGRO   NETHERLANDS

NORWAY   POLAND   PORTUGAL   ROMANIA   RUSSIA

Miles
0   200   400   600   800   1,000
0   400   800   1,200   1,600
Kilometers

Atlantic Ocean

Arctic Ocean

Arctic Circle

ICELAND

SWEDEN   FINLAND

NORWAY

ESTONIA

LATVIA

DENMARK   LITHUANIA

RUSSIA   RUSSIA

UNITED KINGDOM

IRELAND

BELARUS

NETHERLANDS   POLAND

GERMANY

BELGIUM   1   CZECH REPUBLIC

2   SLOVAKIA   UKRAINE

FRANCE   AUSTRIA   HUNGARY

SWITZERLAND   3   CROATIA   ROMANIA

4   6   MOLDOVA

ANDORRA   ITALY   SERBIA

MONACO   7   BULGARIA

5   TURKEY

SPAIN   GREECE   MACEDONIA

ALBANIA

PORTUGAL   MALTA

1. LUXEMBOURG
2. LIECHTENSTEIN
3. SLOVENIA
4. SAN MARINO
5. VATICAN CITY
6. BOSNIA & HERZEGOVINA
7. MONTENEGRO

N
W   E
S

SAN MARINO   SERBIA   SLOVAKIA   SLOVENIA   SPAIN   SWEDEN

SWITZERLAND   TURKEY   UKRAINE   UNITED KINGDOM   VATICAN CITY

7

Landforms

Europe has many different types of landforms, including plateaus, plains, highlands, and many mountain ranges.

Along Europe's eastern border lie the great Ural Mountains. They divide Europe from Asia. Other high mountain ranges, such as the Alps, the Pyrenees, and the Caucasus, create natural borders between countries.

Low-lying land

Most of the land in the Netherlands is below sea level. Long canals drain water from the flat, low-lying land. Without the canals, the land would be flooded by rain.

Northern European Plain

The Northern European Plain is one of the largest plains in the world. It stretches from the Pyrenees Mountains on the France-Spain border, across northern Europe, to the Ural Mountains of Russia. The land is mostly flat, with some hilly areas, including the Central Russian Uplands.

A smoking mountain

Mount Etna, on the Italian island of Sicily, is the tallest active volcano in Europe. A volcano is a type of mountain. It throws smoke, ash, and red-hot lava high into the air.

Mount Etna erupts on the island of Sicily, Italy.

The Meseta

A huge plateau called the Meseta lies in the heart of Spain. Its average elevation (height) is 2,000 feet (610 meters) above sea level. The high, dry land of the Meseta covers about 40 percent of the Iberian Peninsula.

- The Kjolen Mountains of northern Europe are about half as tall as the Alps.
- Russia's Mount Elbrus is the highest mountain peak in Europe.
- The Caucasus Mountains form a bridge between the Black Sea and the Caspian Sea.
- The Italian peninsula is shaped like a boot.

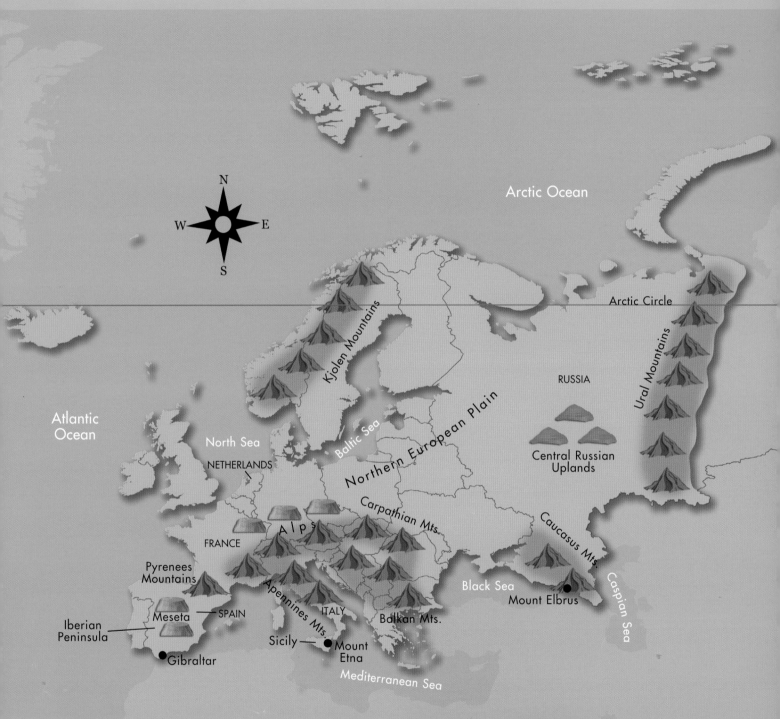

Arctic Ocean

N
W   E
S

Arctic Circle

Kjölen Mountains

RUSSIA

Ural Mountains

Atlantic Ocean

North Sea

NETHERLANDS

Baltic Sea

Northern European Plain

Central Russian Uplands

Alps

Carpathian Mts.

FRANCE

Pyrenees Mountains

Apennines Mts.

Caucasus Mts.

Black Sea

Mount Elbrus

Caspian Sea

Iberian Peninsula

Meseta   SPAIN

ITALY

Balkan Mts.

Sicily   Mount Etna

Gibraltar

Mediterranean Sea

Gibraltar is a strip of land that ends in a limestone cliff. The Rock overlooks the narrow stretch of water separating Spain and Gibraltar from North Africa.

The Rock of Gibraltar

The Alps are the highest mountains in western Europe.

Snow covers some of the Alps' peaks year-round.

9

Bodies of Water

Europe is bordered by two oceans: the Arctic Ocean to the north and the Atlantic Ocean to the west. It's bordered by five seas, as well: the North Sea, the Baltic Sea, the Mediterranean Sea, the Black Sea, and the Caspian Sea.

The continent also has many long rivers and thousands of lakes.

The Rhine River

The Rhine is a very long river. It flows from Switzerland, through Germany and the Netherlands, to the North Sea. It is one of the most important waterways in Europe. It is connected to other major rivers in Europe by man-made canals.

Fjords

Fjords are steep-sided, narrow waterways that stretch inland. These valleys were carved out of the rock by glaciers more than 10,000 years ago. When the ice melted, the sea level rose, and the valleys filled with water.

The fjords in western Norway are some of the most beautiful places in Europe.

The Rhine River snakes past some of Germany's castles.

Venetian boats called gondolas carry people around Venice.

Venice

Venice, Italy, is built on islands in the middle of a lagoon. A system of canals connects the islands.

- Finland has about 60,000 lakes, many with rocky islands in the middle.
- The Loire is France's longest river. It flows through rolling countryside and past large castles.

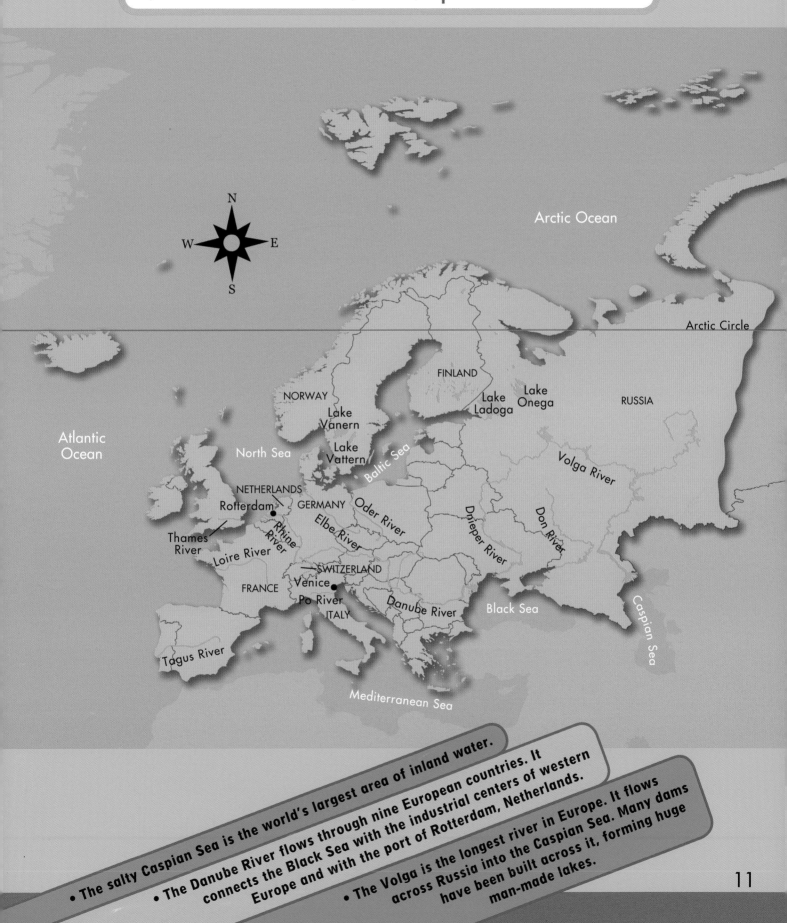

Arctic Ocean

N
W   E
S

Arctic Circle

FINLAND

NORWAY

Lake
Vanern

Lake
Ladoga

Lake
Onega

RUSSIA

Atlantic
Ocean

North Sea

Lake
Vattern

Baltic Sea

Volga River

NETHERLANDS

Rotterdam

GERMANY

Oder River

Rhine
River

Elbe River

Dnieper River

Don River

Thames
River

Loire River

SWITZERLAND

FRANCE

Venice

Po River

ITALY

Danube River

Black Sea

Caspian Sea

Tagus River

Mediterranean Sea

- The salty Caspian Sea is the world's largest area of inland water.
- The Danube River flows through nine European countries. It connects the Black Sea with the industrial centers of western Europe and with the port of Rotterdam, Netherlands.
- The Volga is the longest river in Europe. It flows across Russia into the Caspian Sea. Many dams have been built across it, forming huge man-made lakes.

Climate

Although much of Europe lies closer to the Arctic Circle than to the equator, the continent's climate is fairly warm.

The reason is that the seas around Europe's coasts are warmed by special ocean currents.

Climate is the average weather a place has from season to season, year to year. Rainfall and temperature play large parts in a region's climate.

Land of the Midnight Sun

Part of Sweden lies north of the Arctic Circle. This area is called the Land of the Midnight Sun. The sun shines almost 24 hours a day there in late June and early July. In December and January, however, the sky is dark all day, and temperatures turn very cold.

A time-lapse photo of the midnight sun over northern Sweden in the summer

Mediterranean warmth

Countries around the Mediterranean Sea enjoy hot, dry summers and warm, wet winters. Winds blowing from the south bring warmth from the equator. Inland seas, such as the Mediterranean, also trap warmth from the sun. The seas stay warm because there are no strong ocean waves to cool them.

The warm waters of the Mediterranean coast

Climate basics

A region's climate depends upon three major things: how close it is to the ocean, how high up it is, and how close it is to the equator. Areas along the ocean have milder climates than areas farther inland. The higher a region is, and the farther it is from the equator, the colder its temperature.

- In Belgium, it rains an average of 208 days per year.
- Most of Norway's coastline lies near or within the Arctic Circle. But much of it has no ice or snow, even in the winter. Warm ocean winds keep ice and snow from forming.

Climate

_____ country boundary

dry — dry most or all year with hot summers and warm to cold winters

polar — dry and cold all year

mountain — wet and dry seasons, cool to cold all year

mild — wet winters or all year with warm to hot summers and cool winters

continental — wet, warm to hot summers and cold winters

N
W E
S

Arctic Ocean

Arctic Circle

SWEDEN

NORWAY

Atlantic Ocean

North Sea

Baltic Sea

BELGIUM

UKRAINE

Black Sea

Caspian Sea

Mediterranean Sea

- About 20 to 60 inches (51 to 152 centimeters) of precipitation fall on most of the European continent each year.

- Regions that lie on the western side of Europe's mountains are the wettest regions on the continent. They can receive more than 80 inches (203 cm) of precipitation each year.

- The average winter temperature in northern Ukraine is 21 degrees Fahrenheit (minus 6 degrees Celsius).

13

Plants

Most plants on the European continent are well-adapted to the forest ecosystem. An ecosystem is all of the living and nonliving things in a certain area. It includes plants, animals, soil, weather ... everything!

On the grasslands of southeastern Europe, the soil is rich, but there aren't many trees. Tough grasses grow there. Wildflowers grow in the fields, forests, and mountain valleys of the milder West. Olive trees and vines grow best along the coasts of the warm Mediterranean Sea.

Some Plants of Europe

forest

olive tree	The olive tree is native to the Mediterranean region. It can live for 500 years and grow back even after it has been chopped down.
pine tree	Pine trees are a type of evergreen tree called a conifer. They have needle-like leaves and produce cones.
tulip	Tulips come in every color except blue and true black. The Netherlands is well-known for growing tulips.
wildflowers	The forests and grasslands of western Europe are carpeted with wildflowers. The United Kingdom has about 1,500 different wildflower species.

mountain

gentian — The gentian is a very hardy flower that grows well in the cold mountain regions of Europe. Its blooms are usually blue or purple.

wetlands

fern — Ferns grow well in dark, wet conditions. Their leaves are called fronds.

cattails — Cattails are tall wetland plants with fuzzy, brown seed heads. Their stems and leaves provide shelter and food for many kinds of birds and fish.

tundra

moss — Moss is one of the few plants hardy enough to survive the long, cold tundra winters.

Major Ecosystems

— country boundary

desert	grassland	mountain	wetlands
forest	ice cap	tundra	

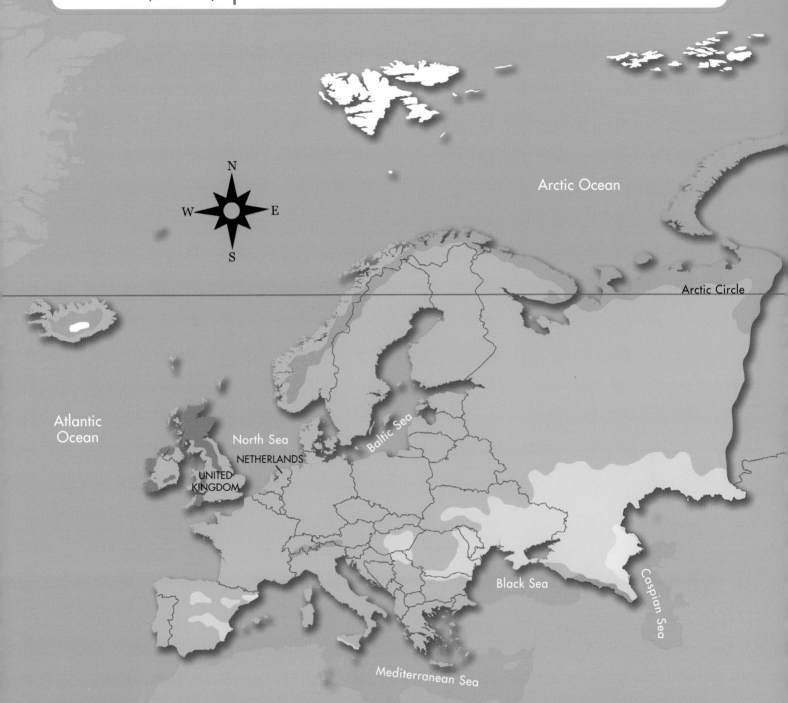

Arctic Ocean

Arctic Circle

Atlantic Ocean

North Sea

NETHERLANDS

UNITED KINGDOM

Baltic Sea

Black Sea

Caspian Sea

Mediterranean Sea

Animals

Although a variety of ecosystems exist in Europe, the forest ecosystem is the largest. An ecosystem is all of the living and nonliving things in a certain area.

Small animals such as rabbits, foxes, and badgers live in the forests of western Europe. Pine martens and wolverines live in the North. Wild boars and lynxs are two of the larger animals living in the forests of eastern Europe.

Some Animals of Europe

forest		
deer	Deer feed on leaves and herbs and chew the bark of trees.
pine marten	The pine marten is a cat-sized animal with chestnut-brown fur, a creamy-yellow throat, and a long, bushy tail.
wild boar	The wild boar searches for roots just beneath the forest floor.
wolverine	The wolverine is a relative of the weasel. It's a shy animal, but it can be a fierce hunter.
bear	The brown bear lives in the forests of northeastern Europe. It feeds on berries, fish, and small animals.
gray wolf	Gray wolves live in the forests of northern and eastern Europe. They can also be found in tundra and mountain ecosystems.

mountain		
golden eagle	When diving to catch its prey, the golden eagle can reach speeds of up to 200 miles (320 kilometers) an hour.
Iberian lynx	The Iberian lynx is a mountain cat found only in Europe. It leaps down on its prey from the trees.
ibex	The deer-like ibex climbs easily over rocky mountain slopes.

tundra		
mountain hare	The mountain hare's brown summer fur turns mostly white in the winter. This change allows the hare to hide from predators in the snow.
reindeer	Both male and female reindeer have antlers. Antlers are shed (dropped) and regrown each year.

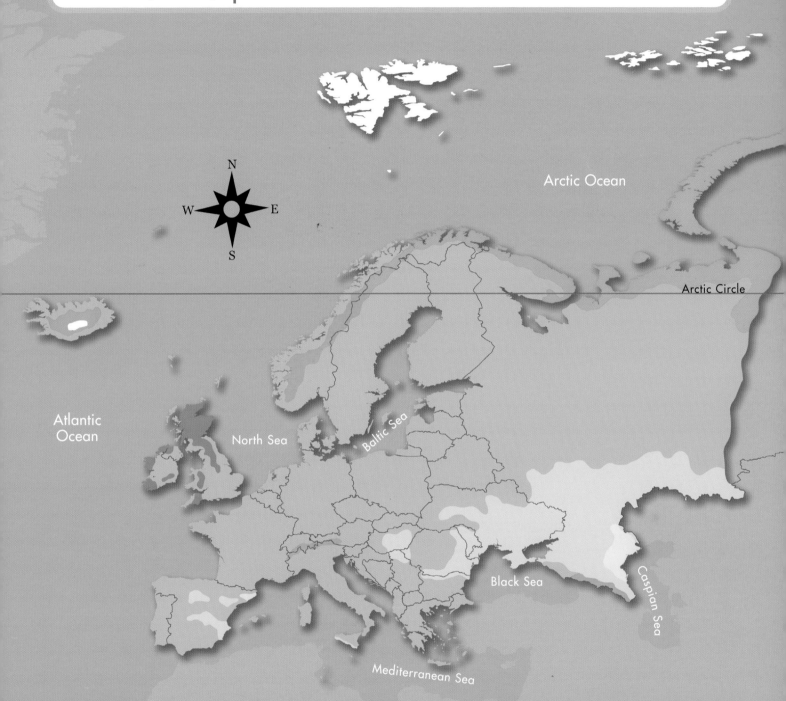

Major Ecosystems

—— country boundary

desert | grassland | mountain | wetlands
forest | ice cap | tundra

Arctic Ocean

N
W   E
S

Arctic Circle

Atlantic
Ocean

North Sea

Baltic Sea

Black Sea

Caspian Sea

Mediterranean Sea

Population

Compared to the other six continents, Europe is very crowded. It has the third-largest population, even though it is almost the smallest in land size.

People come to Europe's cities to work. As a result, Europe's population is large and growing quickly.

A European "family"

The European Union, or EU, is a group that was set up so European countries could trade easily with each other. Today, it is a growing "family" that works together to do more than just trade. More than half of all European countries belong to the EU. They use one common money system called the Euro.

Mountain villages

Few people live in Europe's mountain regions. Transportation is difficult, and the winters can be bitterly cold and snowy.

A village nestled in an Austrian mountain valley

Four big cities

Europe has some of the world's oldest and most famous cities. Tourists come from all over the world to visit its historical sites and museums.

London, United Kingdom, has nearly 7.5 million people. Many different cultures from all over the world make the city an exciting place to live.

Paris, France, has been a center of literature, art, and music for hundreds of years. More than 2 million people live in Paris, with another 10 million people living in the nearby suburbs.

One of Paris' most famous sites, the Eiffel Tower

Moscow is the capital of Russia, the country's most populated city, and the most populated city in Europe. About 11 million people live in Moscow.

The famous domes of St. Basil's Cathedral, a symbol of Moscow

With about 3.5 million people, **Berlin** is the most populated city in Germany. The German capital is famous for its festivals and nightlife.

• For its size, Iceland is one of the world's least populated countries. It averages just seven people per square mile.

• Many people live along Italy's coasts because of the warm Mediterranean climate.

• The total population of Lithuania is 3.5 million people. This about the same number of people that live in the city of Berlin, Germany.

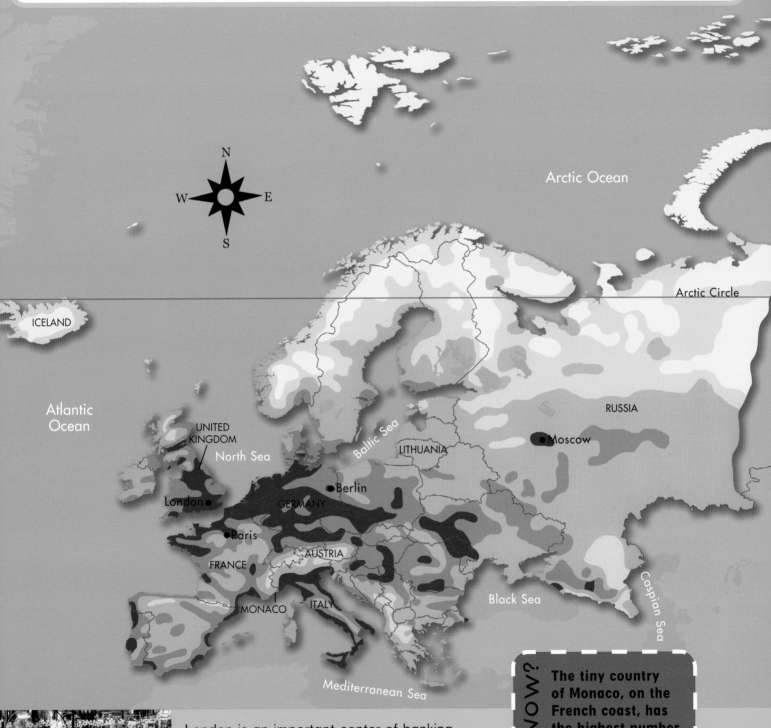

People per Square Mile

| less than **5** | **5-25** | **25-125** | **125-250** | more than **250** |

● place of interest
—— country boundary

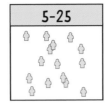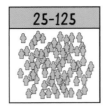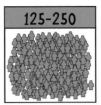

N **W** **E** **S**

Arctic Ocean

Arctic Circle

ICELAND

Atlantic Ocean

RUSSIA

●Moscow

UNITED KINGDOM

North Sea

Baltic Sea

LITHUANIA

London●

●Berlin

GERMANY

●Paris

AUSTRIA

FRANCE

Black Sea

MONACO

ITALY

Caspian Sea

Mediterranean Sea

London is an important center of banking, business, and entertainment. It is the most populated city in the United Kingdom.

London bustles with activity both day and night.

DID YOU KNOW? The tiny country of Monaco, on the French coast, has the highest number of people living in the smallest area in the world.

People and Customs

Europe is home to many different peoples and cultures. In every European country, a part of the population is made up of people from other regions.

Most European countries have very strong traditions. A country's art, food, religion, and sports are all sources of pride.

The Roma

The Roma people first came from India around 1,000 years ago. Today they live all over the world. The Roma are divided into groups, often called tribes or nations. One group, the Spanish Gitano, brought flamenco music and dancing to Spain.

Spanish Gitano in traditional dress

The Sami

The Sami people live in the far north of Norway, Sweden, Finland, and part of Russia. Some live in villages. Others live as nomads, moving their reindeer from place to place in search of fresh pastureland.

The Sami people raise reindeer for their meat, milk, and skins.

Swiss farmers

In summer, many Swiss farmers leave their homes in the valley to drive their cattle up the mountainside. There, the farmers live in cabins, while the cattle graze in pastures.

Cows wear loud bells around their necks so they can be found on the mountainside.

Preparing food

Many European countries have a tradition of preparing food in a special way. In Italy, much of the food is homegrown and very healthy to eat. Many people there still make their own pasta.

A cook flattens pasta dough and cuts it into strips or twists it into shapes. Then it is boiled and eaten with fresh tomatoes, meat, or herbs.

Cheese markets

In the Netherlands, local cheese markets are a favorite tourist attraction. The most popular Dutch cheeses are Edam and Gouda.

Some Dutch cheese-makers entertain tourists by carrying huge wheels of cheese on traditional wooden sleds.

Puppet on a string

"The Adventures of Pinocchio" is a fairy tale by Italian author Carlo Collodi. It tells of a naughty wooden puppet named Pinocchio who one day comes to life. Pinocchio's adventures have become famous all over the world.

Wooden Pinocchio puppets are common in Italian toy stores.

Postcard Places

Europe is filled with wonders of all kinds—from ancient temples to bustling modern cities, from world-famous art museums to tall mountain peaks.

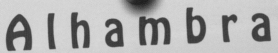

The Arabic fortress of Alhambra, in Granada, Spain, looks out at the Sierra Nevada mountains.

The Colosseum is a huge amphitheater in Rome, Italy. In ancient times, it was used to stage gladiator contests and mock battles.

London
Paris
Prague
Schwangau
Granada
Rome
Athens

The London Eye, in London, United Kingdom, is one of the world's largest observation wheels.

The Acropolis is a rocky hill in the center of Athens, Greece. On its peak stand the remains of an ancient Greek temple called the Parthenon.

Temples of Greece

FAIRY-TALE CASTLES

Germany

Neuschwanstein Castle, near Schwangau, Germany, was the model for Sleeping Beauty's castle in Disneyland (in the U.S. state of California).

Louvre Pyramid

PARIS

PRAGUE

The Louvre Museum, in Paris, France, is one of the oldest in the world, but its glass pyramid entrance is very modern.

The city of Prague, Czech Republic, is full of historic buildings and beautiful bridges.

23

Growing and Making

Europe has many different kinds of industries. Steelmaking is one of the most important. Steel is used to make machinery and cars.

Europe has large supplies of raw materials, such as iron ore, coal, and natural gas. Iron ore is used in manufacturing. Coal and natural gas fuel homes and factories.

Farming is also important. Western Europe, especially, grows a variety of crops, thanks to its mild climate.

Car making

There are many car factories in western Europe. Famous sports cars, such as Ferrari, BMW, and Porsche, are built there. Most cars are built by machines on assembly lines.

Robots do much of the work on a car assembly line.

Oil and natural gas

Romania has a large supply of oil lying beneath it. This oil is pumped up and turned into gasoline, chemicals, man-made fibers, and dyes. Romania also has a large supply of natural gas.

A natural gas processing plant in Romania

Nuclear energy

Because the world's supplies of oil, natural gas, and coal are starting to run out, many European countries are using nuclear energy to power their homes and factories. In France, about 75 percent of the electricity is made from nuclear power.

- Spain and Portugal are the top cork producers in the world. Cork comes from the bark of the cork tree and is used to make shoes, flooring, and bottle stoppers.
- About 80 percent of Russia's exports are oil, natural gas, and metals.
- Italy and Poland are two of the top apple producers in Europe.

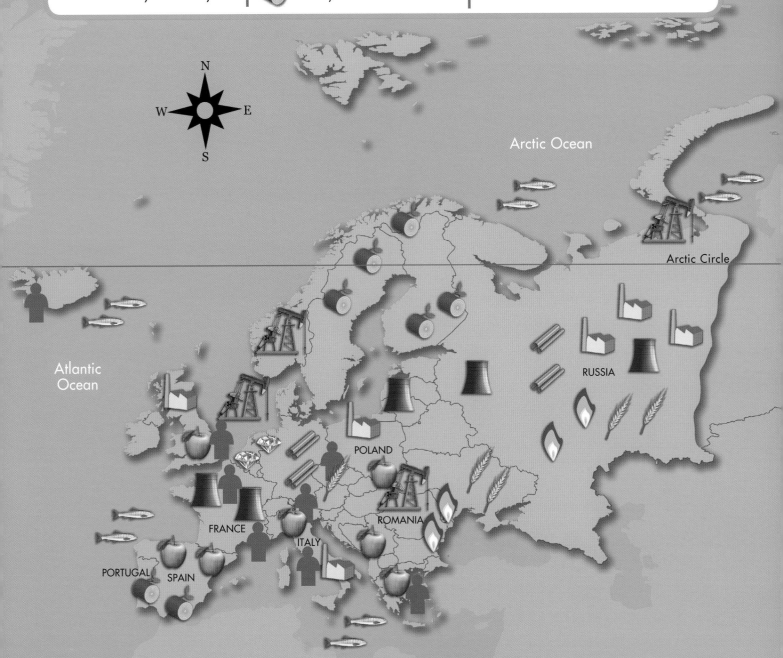

Major Natural Resources, Land Use, and Industry

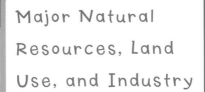

 Manufacturing

Fishing

Natural Gas

Forestry

Oil

Nuclear

Tourism

Mining  diamonds   metal

Farming   fruit   wheat

—— country boundary

Arctic Ocean

Arctic Circle

Atlantic Ocean

RUSSIA

POLAND

ROMANIA

FRANCE

ITALY

PORTUGAL   SPAIN

Fruits and vegetables are grown throughout Europe in greenhouses and plastic tunnels called polytunnels. These structures help farmers grow crops even when the weather is cold. They also help protect crops from insects and disease.

Crops growing in a polytunnel

25

Transportation

Because of Europe's small land size, traveling from country to country is easy.

A large, well-developed railway system connects towns and cities across Europe. Countless major highways provide excellent means of transportation, too.

Europe's many major seaports and airports move goods and people quickly across the continent and around the world.

Canals in the city

Canals lie all over Europe. A canal is a waterway dug across land. The canals of Amsterdam, Netherlands, form rings around the city. Boats can move easily from one area to another. Venice, Italy, and St. Petersburg, Russia, are also famous canal cities.

Foot bridges throughout Amsterdam allow walkers and bicyclists to cross canals easily.

On the road

Thousands of trucks travel on European highways every day, carrying animals, food, cars, and other goods. Special trucks called tankers carry chemicals, oil, or gasoline.

The TGV

The French Train à Grande Vitesse (TGV) is one of the world's fastest trains. It takes people across France at an average speed of 188 miles (300 kilometers) per hour. *Train à Grande Vitesse* means "high-speed train" in French.

The French TGV is shaped like a bullet.

Largest port

Rotterdam, Netherlands, is the largest port in Europe. Many of the ships that use the port are container ships. Goods are piled high in sealed containers on these huge, barge-like ships, which sail from ports in Asia for several weeks.

- The largest ports on the Black Sea include Varna, Bulgaria; Constanta, Romania; and Odesa, Ukraine.
- Marseille is the second-largest city in France (after Paris) and one of the busiest ports on the Mediterranean Sea.

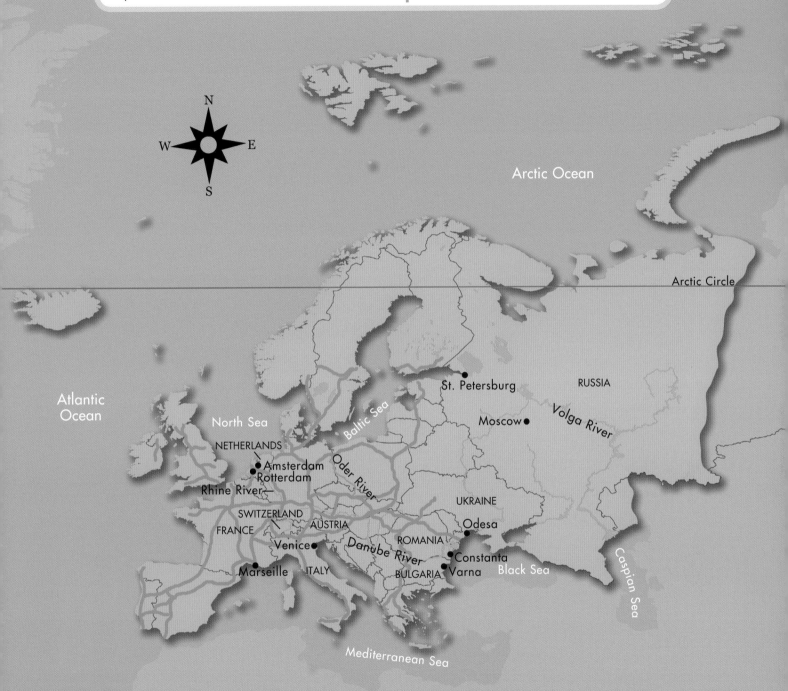

Major Transportation Routes

N
W   E
S

Arctic Ocean

Arctic Circle

St. Petersburg

RUSSIA

Moscow ●

Volga River

Atlantic Ocean

Baltic Sea

North Sea

NETHERLANDS

● Amsterdam
● Rotterdam

Oder River

Rhine River—

SWITZERLAND

FRANCE

AUSTRIA

UKRAINE

● Odesa

Venice ●

Danube River

ROMANIA

● Constanta

Marseille ●

ITALY

BULGARIA

● Varna

Black Sea

Caspian Sea

Mediterranean Sea

The Moscow Metro, in Russia, is a beautiful subway system. Built in the 1930s, the subway is filled with sculptures and paintings. Today, the Moscow Metro covers more than 170 miles (272 km) and carries 9 million people each day.

Moscow's subway stations are works of art.

Riding the Orient Express

The passengers are in their seats. Their luggage has been loaded. They are traveling from Paris, France, to Venice, Italy, on the Orient Express, Europe's fanciest passenger train. All aboard!

As the railcars leave the station, the steward checks to make sure everyone is comfortable. The train follows a winding river through the rolling French countryside. The passengers watch farms and vineyards whizz by their windows.

After an elegant dinner in the dining car, the passengers settle in for the night. While the passengers sleep, the train keeps rolling. In the morning, it chugs through Switzerland and passes the towering peaks of the Alps. It begins to climb.

Suddenly, the train plunges into the dark Arlberg Tunnel. On the other side lie snow-capped mountains and the city of Innsbruck, Austria.

The train travels south, to the Italian city of Verona. There, passengers get off the train to spend an evening at the opera in a huge, open-air theater called the Roman Amphitheater.

Once everyone is back onboard, the train continues to its final stop: Venice. Through the windows, the passengers watch narrow boats called gondolas glide up and down the canals. In just a few minutes, the train will stop, and the passengers' Italian adventure will begin!

The Orient Express has been making the long journey from one side of Europe to the other for many years. In the beginning, it went all the way from Paris, France, to Istanbul, Turkey. Today, travelers make the shorter trip from Paris to Venice, Italy.

29

Europe At-a-Glance

Continent size: the second-smallest of Earth's seven continents

Number of countries: 44; Russia and Turkey lie in two continents—Europe and Asia

Major languages:
- English
- French
- German
- Greek
- Hungarian
- Italian
- Russian
- Spanish
- Turkish

Total population: 729 million (2005 estimate)

Largest country (land size): Russia

Most populated country: Russia

Most populated city: Moscow, Russia

Climate: mostly mild in the West and continental (wet, warm to hot summers and cold winters) in the East; dry and cold all year in the far North; dry in the southeastern and southwestern regions; cool to cold in the mountains

Highest point: Mount Elbrus, Russia, 18,619 feet (5,679 meters)

Lowest point: northern shore of the Caspian Sea, 92 feet (28 m) below sea level

Longest river: Volga River

Largest body of water: Caspian Sea

Largest desert: Europe is the only continent with no deserts

Major agricultural products:
- barley
- beans
- citrus fruits
- corn
- dairy products
- goats
- grapes
- oats
- olives
- peas
- pigs
- potatoes
- poultry
- rye
- sheep
- sugar beets
- wheat

Major industries:
- agriculture
- forestry
- fishing
- mining
- manufacturing (clothing, iron, steel, ships, motor vehicles, railroad equipment, chemicals, and electronic equipment)

Natural resources:
- bauxite
- coal
- copper
- iron ore
- manganese
- natural gas
- nickel
- oil
- steel

Glossary

body of water – a mass of water that is in one area; such as a river, lake, or ocean

boundary – a line that shows the border of a country, state, or other land area

canal – a waterway dug across land

climate – the average weather a place has from season to season, year to year

compass rose – a symbol used to show direction on a map

continent – one of seven large land masses on Earth, including Africa, Antarctica, Asia, Australia, Europe, North America, and South America

crops – plants that are grown in large amounts and are used for food or income

current – a part of a body of water that is moving in a path

desert – a hot or cold, very dry area that has few plants growing on it

ecosystem – all of the living and nonliving things in a certain area, including plants, animals, soil, and weather

equator – an imaginary line around Earth; it divides the northern and southern hemispheres

fjord – a steep-sided, narrow waterway that stretches inland

forest – land covered by trees and plants

glacier – a huge, slow-moving mass of ice

grassland – land covered mostly with grass

highland – high or hilly land

island – land that is completely surrounded by water

lagoon – a shallow body of water that lies near or is connected to a larger body of water

lake – a body of water that is completely surrounded by land

landform – a natural feature on Earth's surface

legend – the part of a map that explains the meaning of the map's symbols

lowland – low or flat land

mountain – a mass of land that rises high above the land that surrounds it

natural resources – materials such as water, trees, and minerals that are found in nature

North Pole – the northern-most point on Earth

nuclear energy – power that is made by the center (nucleus) of an atom (the smallest bit of matter)

ocean – the large body of saltwater that covers most of Earth's surface

peninsula – a body of land that is surrounded by water on three sides

plain – an area of flat or nearly flat land

plateau – a large, flat, and often rocky area of land that is higher than the surrounding land

population – the total number of people who live in one area

port – a place where ships can load or unload cargo (goods or people)

precipitation – water that falls from the sky in the form of rain, snow, sleet, or hail

river – a large stream of water that empties into a lake, ocean, or other river

scale – the size of a map or model compared to the actual size of things they stand for

South Pole – the southern-most point on Earth

temperature – how hot or cold something is

tundra – land with no trees that lies in the arctic regions

valley – a low place between mountains or hills

wetland – an area that has very wet soil and is covered with water at least part of the year

Index

On the Web

FactHound offers a safe, fun way to find Web sites related to topics in this book.
All of the sites on FactHound have been researched by our staff.

1. Visit www.facthound.com
2. Type in this special code: 1404838821
3. Click on the FETCH IT button.

Your trusty FactHound will fetch the best sites for you!

Look for all of the books in the Picture Window Books World Atlases series:

Atlas of Africa

Atlas of Australia

Atlas of Europe

Atlas of North America

Atlas of South America

Atlas of Southwest and Central Asia

Atlas of the Far East and Southeast Asia

Atlas of the Poles and Oceans